OECD/G20 Base Erosion

MW01670655

Guidance on Transfer Pricing Documentation and Country-by-Country Reporting

OECD

BETTER POLICIES FOR BETTER LIVES

This document and any map included herein are without prejudice to the status of or sovereignty over any territory, to the delimitation of international frontiers and boundaries and to the name of any territory, city or area.

Please cite this publication as:
OECD (2014), *Guidance on Transfer Pricing Documentation and Country-by-Country Reporting*, OECD/G20 Base Erosion and Profit Shifting Project, OECD Publishing.
http://dx.doi.org/10.1787/9789264219236-en

ISBN 978-92-64-21922-9 (print)
ISBN 978-92-64-21923-6 (PDF)

Series: OECD/G20 Base Erosion and Profit Shifting Project
ISSN 2313-2604 (print)
ISSN 2313-2612 (online)

Photo credits: Cover © archerix / Fotolia.

Corrigenda to OECD publications may be found on line at: *www.oecd.org/about/publishing/corrigenda.htm*.

Foreword

Addressing base erosion and profit shifting (BEPS) is a key priority of governments around the globe. In 2013, OECD and G20 countries, working together on an equal footing, adopted a 15-point Action Plan to address BEPS. The Action Plan aims to ensure that profits are taxed where economic activities generating the profits are performed and where value is created. It was agreed that addressing BEPS is critical for countries and must be done in a timely manner, not least to prevent the existing consensus-based international tax framework from unravelling, which would increase uncertainty for businesses at a time when cross-border investments are more necessary than ever. As a result, the Action Plan provides for 15 actions to be delivered by 2015, with a number of actions to be delivered in 2014.

The OECD Committee on Fiscal Affairs (CFA), bringing together 44 countries on an equal footing (all OECD members, OECD accession countries, and G20 countries), has adopted a first set of seven deliverables described in the Action Plan and due in 2014. This report is part of these deliverables and is an output of Action 13.

Developing countries and other non-OECD/non-G20 economies have been extensively consulted through regional and global fora meetings and their input has been fed into the work. Business representatives, trade unions, civil society organisations and academics have also been very involved through opportunities to comment on discussion drafts. These have generated more than 3 500 pages of comments and were discussed at five public consultation meetings and via three webcasts that attracted more than 10 000 viewers.

The first set of reports and recommendations, delivered in 2014, addresses seven of the actions in the BEPS Action Plan published in July 2013. Given the Action Plan's aim of providing comprehensive and coherent solutions to BEPS, the proposed measures, while agreed, are not yet formally finalised. They may be affected by some of the decisions to be taken with respect to the 2015 deliverables with which the 2014 deliverable will interact. They do reflect consensus, as of July 2014, on a number of solutions to put an end to BEPS.

The adoption of this first set of deliverables and the implementation of the relevant measures by national governments mean that: hybrid mismatches will be neutralised; treaty shopping and other forms of treaty abuse will be addressed; abuse of transfer pricing rules in the key area of intangibles will be greatly minimised; and country-by-country reporting will provide governments with information on the global allocation of the profits, economic activity and taxes of MNEs. Equally, OECD and G20 countries have agreed upon a report concluding that it is feasible to implement BEPS measures through a multilateral instrument. They have also advanced the work to fight harmful tax practices, in particular in the area of IP regimes and tax rulings. Finally, they have reached a common understanding of the challenges raised by the digital economy, which will now allow them to deepen their work in this area, one in which BEPS is exacerbated.

By its nature, BEPS requires co-ordinated responses. This is why countries are investing time and resources in developing shared solutions to common problems. At the same time, countries retain their sovereignty over tax matters and measures may be implemented in different countries in different ways, as long as they do not conflict with countries' international legal commitments.

Table of contents

Abbreviations and acronyms

APA	Advance pricing agreement
BEPS	Base erosion and profit shifting
CFA	Committee on Fiscal Affairs
FTE	Full-time equivalent
MNE	Multinational enterprise
OECD	Organisation for Economic Co-operation and Development
PE	Permanent establishment
R&D	Research and development
SME	Small and medium enterprise

Executive summary

Action 13 of the *Action Plan on Base Erosion and Profit Shifting* (OECD, 2013) recognises that enhancing transparency for tax administrations by providing them with adequate information to conduct transfer pricing risk assessments and examinations is an essential part of tackling the base erosion and profit shifting (BEPS) problem. This document contains revised standards for transfer pricing documentation and a template for country-by-country reporting of income, earnings, taxes paid and certain measures of economic activity.

The country-by-country report requires multinational enterprises (MNEs) to report annually and for each tax jurisdiction in which they do business the amount of revenue, profit before income tax and income tax paid and accrued. It also requires MNEs to report their total employment, capital, retained earnings and tangible assets in each tax jurisdiction. Finally, it requires MNEs to identify each entity within the group doing business in a particular tax jurisdiction and to provide an indication of the business activities each entity engages in.

The guidance on transfer pricing documentation requires MNEs to provide tax administrations high-level global information regarding their global business operations and transfer pricing policies in a "master file" that would be available to all relevant country tax administrations. It also requires that more transactional transfer pricing documentation be provided in a local file in each country, identifying relevant related party transactions, the amounts involved in those transactions, and the company's analysis of the transfer pricing determinations they have made with regard to those transactions.

Taken together, these three documents (country-by-country report, master file and local file) will require taxpayers to articulate consistent transfer pricing positions, will provide tax administrations with useful information to assess transfer pricing risks, make determinations about where audit resources can most effectively be deployed, and, in the event audits are called for, provide information to commence and target audit enquiries. This information should make it easier for tax administrations to identify whether companies have engaged in transfer pricing and other practices that have the effect of artificially shifting substantial amounts of income into tax-advantaged environments. The countries participating in the BEPS Project agree that these new reporting provisions, and the transparency they will encourage, will contribute to the objective of understanding, controlling, and tackling BEPS behaviours.

The specific content of the various documents reflects an effort to balance tax administration information needs, concerns about inappropriate use of the information, and the compliance costs and burdens imposed on business. Some countries would strike that balance in a different way by requiring reporting in the country-by-country report of additional transactional data (beyond that available in the master file and local file for transactions of entities operating in their jurisdictions) regarding related party interest payments, royalty payments and especially related party service fees. Countries expressing this view are primarily those from emerging markets (Argentina, Brazil, China, Colombia, India, Mexico, South Africa, and Turkey) who state they need such information to perform risk assessment and who find it challenging to obtain information on the global operations of an MNE group headquartered elsewhere. Other countries expressed support for the way in which the balance has been struck in this document. Taking all these views into account, it is mandated that countries participating in the BEPS project will carefully review the implementation of these new standards and will reassess no later than the end of 2020 whether modifications to the content of these reports should be made to require reporting of additional or different data.

Effective implementation of the new reporting standards and reporting rules will be essential. Additional work will be undertaken over the next several months to identify the most appropriate means of filing the required information with and disseminating it to tax administrations. In that work, due regard will be given to considerations related to protection of the confidentiality of the information required by the reporting standards, the need for making the information available on a timely basis to all relevant countries, and other relevant factors.

Bibliography

OECD (2013), *Action Plan on Base Erosion and Profit Shifting*, OECD Publishing.
http://dx.doi.org/10.1787/9789264202719-en

Chapter V

Documentation

The text of Chapter V of the Transfer Pricing Guidelines is deleted in its entirety and replaced with the following language and annexes.

A. Introduction

1. This chapter provides guidance for tax administrations to take into account in developing rules and/or procedures on documentation to be obtained from taxpayers in connection with a transfer pricing enquiry or risk assessment. It also provides guidance to assist taxpayers in identifying documentation that would be most helpful in showing that their transactions satisfy the arm's length principle and hence in resolving transfer pricing issues and facilitating tax examinations.

2. When Chapter V of these Guidelines was adopted in 1995, tax administrations and taxpayers had less experience in creating and using transfer pricing documentation. The previous language in Chapter V of the Guidelines put an emphasis on the need for reasonableness in the documentation process from the perspective of both taxpayers and tax administrations, as well as on the desire for a greater level of cooperation between tax administrations and taxpayers in addressing documentation issues in order to avoid excessive documentation compliance burdens while at the same time providing for adequate information to apply the arm's length principle reliably. The previous language of Chapter V did not provide for a list of documents to be included in a transfer pricing documentation package nor did it provide clear guidance with respect to the link between the process for documenting transfer pricing, the administration of penalties and the burden of proof.

3. Since then, many countries have adopted transfer pricing documentation rules and the proliferation of these requirements, combined with a dramatic increase in the volume and complexity of international intra-group trade and the heightened scrutiny of transfer pricing issues by tax

administrations, has resulted in a significant increase in compliance costs for taxpayers. Nevertheless tax administrations often find transfer pricing documentation to be less than fully informative and not adequate for their tax enforcement and risk assessment needs.

4. The following discussion identifies three objectives of transfer pricing documentation rules. The discussion also provides guidance for the development of such rules so that transfer pricing compliance is more straightforward and more consistent among countries, while at the same time providing tax administrations with more focused and useful information for transfer pricing risk assessments and audits. An important overarching consideration in developing such rules is to balance the usefulness of the data to tax administrations for transfer pricing risk assessment and other purposes with any increased compliance burdens placed on taxpayers. In this respect it is noted that clear and widely adopted documentation rules can reduce compliance costs which could otherwise arise in a transfer pricing dispute.

B. Objectives of transfer pricing documentation requirements

5. Three objectives of transfer pricing documentation are:

1. to ensure that taxpayers give appropriate consideration to transfer pricing requirements in establishing prices and other conditions for transactions between associated enterprises and in reporting the income derived from such transactions in their tax returns;
2. to provide tax administrations with the information necessary to conduct an informed transfer pricing risk assessment; and
3. to provide tax administrations with useful information to employ in conducting an appropriately thorough audit of the transfer pricing practices of entities subject to tax in their jurisdiction, although it may be necessary to supplement the documentation with additional information as the audit progresses.

6. Each of these objectives should be considered in designing appropriate domestic transfer pricing documentation requirements. It is important that taxpayers be required to carefully evaluate, at or before the time of filing a tax return, their own compliance with the applicable transfer pricing rules. It is also important that tax administrations be able to access the information they need to conduct a transfer pricing risk assessment to make an informed decision about whether to perform an audit. In addition, it is important that tax administrations be able to access or demand, on a timely basis, all additional information necessary to conduct a comprehensive audit once the decision to conduct such an audit is made.

B.1. Taxpayer's assessment of its compliance with the arm's length principle

7. By requiring taxpayers to articulate convincing, consistent and cogent transfer pricing positions, transfer pricing documentation can help to ensure that a culture of compliance is created. Well-prepared documentation will give tax administrations some assurance that the taxpayer has analysed the positions it reports on tax returns, has considered the available comparable data, and has reached consistent transfer pricing positions. Moreover, contemporaneous documentation requirements will help to ensure the integrity of the taxpayers' positions and restrain taxpayers from developing justifications for their positions after the fact.

8. This compliance objective may be supported in two important ways. First, tax administrations can require that transfer pricing documentation requirements be satisfied on a contemporaneous basis. This would mean that the documentation would be prepared at the time of the transaction, or in any event, no later than the time of completing and filing the tax return for the fiscal year in which the transaction takes place. The second way to encourage compliance is to establish transfer pricing penalty regimes in a manner intended to reward timely and accurate preparation of transfer pricing documentation and to create incentives for timely, careful consideration of the taxpayer's transfer pricing positions. Filing requirements and penalty provisions related to documentation are discussed in greater detail in Section D, below.

9. While ideally taxpayers will use transfer pricing documentation as an opportunity to articulate a well thought-out basis for their transfer pricing policies, thereby meeting an important objective of such requirements, issues such as costs, time constraints, and competing demands for the attention of relevant personnel can sometimes undermine these objectives. It is therefore important for countries to keep documentation requirements reasonable and focused on material transactions in order to ensure mindful attention to the most important matters.

B.2. Transfer pricing risk assessment

10. Effective risk identification and assessment constitute an essential early stage in the process of selecting appropriate cases for transfer pricing audits or enquiries and in focusing such audits on the most important issues. Because tax administrations operate with limited resources, it is important for them to accurately evaluate, at the very outset of a possible audit, whether a taxpayer's transfer pricing arrangements warrant in-depth review and a commitment of significant tax enforcement resources. Particularly with regard to transfer pricing issues (which generally are complex and fact-

intensive), effective risk assessment becomes an essential prerequisite for a focused and resource-efficient audit. The OECD Handbook on Transfer Pricing Risk Assessment is a useful tool to consider in conducting such risk assessments.

11. Proper assessment of transfer pricing risk by the tax administration requires access to sufficient, relevant and reliable information at an early stage. While there are many sources of relevant information, transfer pricing documentation is one critical source of such information.

12. There is a variety of tools and sources of information used for identifying and evaluating transfer pricing risks of taxpayers and transactions, including transfer pricing forms (to be filed with the annual tax return), transfer pricing mandatory questionnaires focusing on particular areas of risk, general transfer pricing documentation requirements identifying the supporting evidence necessary to demonstrate the taxpayer's compliance with the arm's length principle, and cooperative discussions between tax administrations and taxpayers. Each of the tools and sources of information appears to respond to the same fundamental observation: there is a need for the tax administration to have ready access to relevant information at an early stage to enable an accurate and informed transfer pricing risk assessment. Assuring that a high quality transfer pricing risk assessment can be carried out efficiently and with the right kinds of reliable information should be one important consideration in designing transfer pricing documentation rules.

B.3. Transfer pricing audit

13. A third objective for transfer pricing documentation is to provide tax administrations with useful information to employ in conducting a thorough transfer pricing audit. Transfer pricing audit cases tend to be fact-intensive. They often involve difficult evaluations of the comparability of several transactions and markets. They can require detailed consideration of financial, factual and other industry information. The availability of adequate information from a variety of sources during the audit is critical to facilitating a tax administration's orderly examination of the taxpayer's controlled transactions with associated enterprises and enforcement of the applicable transfer pricing rules.

14. In situations where a proper transfer pricing risk assessment suggests that a thorough transfer pricing audit is warranted with regard to one or more issues, it is clearly the case that the tax administration must have the ability to obtain, within a reasonable period, all of the relevant documents and information in the taxpayer's possession. This includes information regarding the taxpayer's operations and functions, relevant

information on the operations, functions and financial results of associated enterprises with which the taxpayer has entered into controlled transactions, information regarding potential comparables, including internal comparables, and documents regarding the operations and financial results of potentially comparable uncontrolled transactions and unrelated parties. To the extent such information is included in the transfer pricing documentation, special information and document production procedures can potentially be avoided. It must be recognised, however, that it would be unduly burdensome and inefficient for transfer pricing documentation to attempt to anticipate all of the information that might possibly be required for a full audit. Accordingly, situations will inevitably arise when tax administrations wish to obtain information not included in the documentation package. Thus, a tax administration's access to information should not be limited to, or by, the documentation package relied on in a transfer pricing risk assessment. Where a jurisdiction requires particular information to be kept for transfer pricing audit purposes, such requirements should balance the tax administration's need for information and the compliance burdens on taxpayers.

15. It may often be the case that the documents and other information required for a transfer pricing audit will be in the possession of members of the MNE group other than the local affiliate under examination. Often the necessary documents will be located outside the country whose tax administration is conducting the audit. It is therefore important that the tax administration is able to obtain directly or through information sharing, such as exchange of information mechanisms, information that extends beyond the country's borders.

C. A three-tiered approach to transfer pricing documentation

16. In order to achieve the objectives described in Section B, countries should adopt a standardised approach to transfer pricing documentation. This section describes a three-tiered structure consisting of (i) a master file containing standardised information relevant for all MNE group members;(ii) a local file referring specifically to material transactions of the local taxpayer; and (iii) a country-by-country report containing certain information relating to the global allocation of the MNE's income and taxes paid together with certain indicators of the location of economic activity within the MNE group.

17. This approach to transfer pricing documentation will provide tax administrations with relevant and reliable information to perform an efficient and robust transfer pricing risk assessment analysis. It will also provide a platform on which the information necessary for an audit can be

developed and provide taxpayers with a means and an incentive to meaningfully consider and describe their compliance with the arm's length principle in material transactions.

C.1. Master file

18. The master file should provide an overview of the MNE group business, including the nature of its global business operations, its overall transfer pricing policies, and its global allocation of income and economic activity in order to assist tax administrations in evaluating the presence of significant transfer pricing risk. In general, the master file is intended to provide a high-level overview in order to place the MNE group's transfer pricing practices in their global economic, legal, financial and tax context. It is not intended to require exhaustive listings of minutiae (*e.g.* a listing of every patent owned by members of the MNE group) as this would be both unnecessarily burdensome and inconsistent with the objectives of the master file. In producing the master file, including lists of important agreements, intangibles and transactions, taxpayers should use prudent business judgment in determining the appropriate level of detail for the information supplied, keeping in mind the objective of the master file to provide tax administrations a high-level overview of the MNE's global operations and policies. When the requirements of the master file can be fully satisfied by specific cross-references to other existing documents, such cross- references, together with copies of the relevant documents, should be deemed to satisfy the relevant requirement. For purposes of producing the master file, information is considered important if its omission would affect the reliability of the transfer pricing outcomes.

19. The information required in the master file provides a "blueprint" of the MNE group and contains relevant information that can be grouped in five categories: a) the MNE group's organisational structure; b) a description of the MNE's business or businesses; c) the MNE's intangibles; d) the MNE's intercompany financial activities; and (e) the MNE's financial and tax positions.

20. Taxpayers should present the information in the master file for the MNE as a whole. However, organisation of the information presented by line of business is permitted where well justified by the facts, *e.g.* where the structure of the MNE group is such that some significant business lines operate largely independently or are recently acquired. Where line of business presentation is used, care should be taken to assure that centralised group functions and transactions between business lines are properly described in the master file. Even where line of business presentation is selected, the entire master file consisting of all business lines should be

available to each country in order to assure that an appropriate overview of the MNE group's global business is provided.

21. Annex I to Chapter V of these Guidelines sets out the information to be included in the master file.

C.2. Local file

22. In contrast to the master file, which provides a high-level overview as described in paragraph 18, the local file provides more detailed information relating to specific intercompany transactions. The information required in the local file supplements the master file and helps to meet the objective of assuring that the taxpayer has complied with the arm's length principle in its material transfer pricing positions affecting a specific jurisdiction. The local file focuses on information relevant to the transfer pricing analysis related to transactions taking place between a local country affiliate and associated enterprises in different countries and which are material in the context of the local country's tax system. Such information would include relevant financial information regarding those specific transactions, a comparability analysis, and the selection and application of the most appropriate transfer pricing method. Where a requirement of the local file can be fully satisfied by a specific cross-reference to information contained in the master file, such a cross-reference should suffice.

23. Annex II to Chapter V of these Guidelines sets out the items of information to be included in the local file.

C.3. Country-by-Country report

24. The country-by-country report requires aggregate tax jurisdiction-wide information relating to the global allocation of the income, the taxes paid, and certain indicators of the location of economic activity among tax jurisdictions in which the MNE group operates. The report also requires a listing of all the Constituent Entities for which financial information is reported, including the tax jurisdiction of incorporation, where different from the tax jurisdiction of residence, as well as the nature of the main business activities carried out by that Constituent Entity.

25. The country-by-country report will be helpful for high-level transfer pricing risk assessment purposes. It may also be used by tax administrations in evaluating other BEPS related risks and where appropriate for economic and statistical analysis. However, the information in the country-by-country report should not be used as a substitute for a detailed transfer pricing analysis of individual transactions and prices based on a full functional analysis and a full comparability analysis. The

information in the country-by-country report on its own does not constitute conclusive evidence that transfer prices are or are not appropriate. It should not be used by tax administrations to propose transfer pricing adjustments based on a global formulary apportionment of income.

26. Annex III to Chapter V of these Guidelines contains a model template for the country-by-country report together with its accompanying instructions.

D. Compliance issues

D.1. Contemporaneous documentation

27. Each taxpayer should endeavour to determine transfer prices for tax purposes in accordance with the arm's length principle, based upon information reasonably available at the time of the transaction. Thus, a taxpayer ordinarily should give consideration to whether its transfer pricing is appropriate for tax purposes before the pricing is established and should confirm the arm's length nature of its financial results at the time of filing its tax return.

28. Taxpayers should not be expected to incur disproportionately high costs and burdens in producing documentation. Therefore, tax administrations should balance requests for documentation against the expected cost and administrative burden to the taxpayer of creating it. Where a taxpayer reasonably demonstrates, having regard to the principles of these Guidelines, that either no comparable data exists or that the cost of locating the comparable data would be disproportionately high relative to the amounts at issue, the taxpayer should not be required to incur costs in searching for such data.

D.2. Time frame

29. Practices regarding the timing of the preparation of the documentation differ among countries. Some countries require information to be finalised by the time the tax return is filed. Others require documentation to be in place by the time the audit commences. There is also a variety in practice regarding the amount of time given to taxpayers to respond to specific tax administration requests for documentation and other audit related information requests. These differences in the time requirements for providing information can add to taxpayers' difficulties in setting priorities and in providing the right information to the tax administrations at the right time.

30. The best practice is to require that the local file be finalised no later than the due date for the filing of the tax return for the fiscal year in question. The master file should be reviewed and, if necessary, updated by the tax return due date for the ultimate parent of the MNE group. In countries pursuing policies of auditing transactions as they occur under co-operative compliance programmes, it may be necessary for certain information to be provided in advance of the filing of the tax return.

31. With regard to the country-by-country report, it is recognised that in some instances final statutory financial statements and other financial information that may be relevant for the country-by-country data described in Annex III may not be finalised until after the due date for tax returns in some countries for a given fiscal year. Under the given circumstances, the date for completion of the country-by-country report described in Annex III to Chapter V of these Guidelines may be extended to one year following the last day of the fiscal year of the ultimate parent of the MNE group.

D.3. Materiality

32. Not all transactions that occur between associated enterprises are sufficiently material to require full documentation in the local file. Tax administrations have an interest in seeing the most important information while at the same time they also have an interest in seeing that MNEs are not so overwhelmed with compliance demands that they fail to consider and document the most important items. Thus, individual country transfer pricing documentation requirements based on Annex II to Chapter V of these Guidelines should include specific materiality thresholds that take into account the size and the nature of the local economy, the importance of the MNE group in that economy, and the size and nature of local operating entities, in addition to the overall size and nature of the MNE group. Measures of materiality may be considered in relative terms (*e.g.* transactions not exceeding a percentage of revenue or a percentage of cost measure) or in absolute amount terms (*e.g.* transactions not exceeding a certain fixed amount). Individual countries should establish their own materiality standards for local file purposes, based on local conditions. The materiality standards should be objective standards that are commonly understood and accepted in commercial practice. See paragraph 18 for the materiality standards applicable in completing the master file.

33. A number of countries have introduced in their transfer pricing documentation rules simplification measures which exempt small and medium-sized enterprises (SMEs) from transfer pricing documentation requirements or limit the information required to be provided by such enterprises. In order not to impose on taxpayers costs and burdens disproportionate to the circumstances, it is recommended to not require

SMEs to produce the amount of documentation that might be expected from larger enterprises. However, SMEs should be obliged to provide information and documents about their material cross-border transactions upon a specific request of the tax administration in the course of a tax examination or for transfer pricing risk assessment purposes.

34. For purposes of Annex III to Chapter V of these Guidelines, the country-by-country report should include all tax jurisdictions in which the MNE group has an entity resident for tax purposes, regardless of the size of business operations in that tax jurisdiction.

D.4. Retention of documents

35. Taxpayers should not be obliged to retain documents beyond a reasonable period consistent with the requirements of domestic law at either the parent company or local entity level. However, at times materials and information required in the documentation package (master file, local file and country-by-country report) may be relevant to a transfer pricing enquiry for a subsequent year that is not time barred, for example where taxpayers voluntarily keep such records in relation to long-term contracts, or to determine whether comparability standards relating to the application of a transfer pricing method in that subsequent year are satisfied. Tax administrations should bear in mind the difficulties in locating documents for prior years and should restrict such requests to instances where they have good reason in connection with the transaction under examination for reviewing the documents in question.

36. Because the tax administration's ultimate interest would be satisfied if the necessary documents were submitted in a timely manner when requested by the tax administration in the course of an examination, the way that documentation is stored - whether in paper, electronic form, or in any other system - should be at the discretion of the taxpayer provided that relevant information can promptly be made available to the tax administration in the form specified by the local country rules and practices.

D.5. Frequency of documentation updates

37. It is recommended that transfer pricing documentation be periodically reviewed in order to determine whether functional and economic analyses are still accurate and relevant and to confirm the validity of the applied transfer pricing methodology. In general, the master file, the local file and the country-by-country report should be reviewed and updated annually. It is recognised, however, that in many situations business descriptions, functional analyses, and descriptions of comparables may not change significantly from year to year.

38. In order to simplify compliance burdens on taxpayers, tax administrations may determine, as long as the operating conditions remain unchanged, that the searches in databases for comparables supporting part of the local file be updated every 3 years rather than annually. Financial data for the comparables should nonetheless be updated every year in order to apply the arm's length principle reliably.

D.6. Language

39. The necessity of providing documentation in local language may constitute a complicating factor with respect to transfer pricing compliance to the extent that substantial time and cost may be involved in translating documents. The language in which transfer pricing documentation should be submitted should be established under local laws. Countries are encouraged to permit filing of transfer pricing documentation in commonly used languages where it will not compromise the usefulness of the documents. Where tax administrations believe that translation of documents is necessary, they should make specific requests for translation and provide sufficient time to make such translation as comfortable a burden as possible.

D.7. Penalties

40. Many countries have adopted documentation-related penalties to ensure efficient operation of transfer pricing documentation requirements. They are designed to make non-compliance more costly than compliance. Penalty regimes are governed by the laws of each individual country. Country practices with regard to transfer pricing documentation-related penalties vary widely. The existence of different local country penalty regimes may influence the quality of taxpayers' compliance so that taxpayers could be driven to favour one country over another in their compliance practices.

41. Documentation-related penalties imposed for failure to comply with transfer pricing documentation requirements or failure to timely submit required information are usually civil (or administrative) monetary penalties. These documentation-related penalties are based on a fixed amount that may be assessed for each document missing or for each fiscal year under review, or calculated as a percentage of the related tax understatement ultimately determined, a percentage of the related adjustment to the income, or as a percentage of the amount of the cross-border transactions not documented.

42. Care should be taken not to impose a documentation-related penalty on a taxpayer for failing to submit data to which the MNE group did not have access. However, a decision not to impose documentation-related penalties does not mean that adjustments cannot be made to income where

prices are not consistent with the arm's length principle. The fact that positions are fully documented does not necessarily mean that the taxpayer's positions are correct. Moreover, an assertion by a local entity that other group members are responsible for transfer pricing compliance is not a sufficient reason for that entity to fail to provide required documentation, nor should such an assertion prevent the imposition of documentation-related penalties for failure to comply with documentation rules where the necessary information is not forthcoming.

43. Another way for countries to encourage taxpayers to fulfil transfer pricing documentation requirements is by designing compliance incentives such as penalty protection or a shift in the burden of proof. Where the documentation meets the requirements and is timely submitted, the taxpayer could be exempted from tax penalties or subject to a lower penalty rate if a transfer pricing adjustment is made and sustained, notwithstanding the provision of documentation. In some jurisdictions where the taxpayer bears the burden of proof regarding transfer pricing matters, a shift of the burden of proof to the tax administration's side where adequate documentation is provided on a timely basis offers another measure that could be used to create an incentive for transfer pricing documentation compliance.

D.8 Confidentiality

44. Tax administrations should take all reasonable steps to ensure that there is no public disclosure of confidential information (trade secrets, scientific secrets, *etc.*) and other commercially sensitive information contained in the documentation package (master file, local file and country-by-country report). Tax administrations should also assure taxpayers that the information presented in transfer pricing documentation will remain confidential. In cases where disclosure is required in public court proceedings or judicial decisions, every effort should be made to ensure that confidentiality is maintained and that information is disclosed only to the extent needed.

45. The OECD Guide "Keeping It Safe" on the protection of confidentiality of information exchanged for tax purposes provides guidance on the rules and practices that must be in place to ensure the confidentiality of tax information exchanged under exchange of information instruments.

D.9. Other issues

46. The requirement to use the most reliable information will usually, but not always, require the use of local comparables over the use of regional comparables where such local comparables are reasonably available. The

use of regional comparables in transfer pricing documentation prepared for countries in the same geographic region in situations where appropriate local comparables are available will not, in some cases, comport with the obligation to rely on the most reliable information. While the simplification benefits of limiting the number of comparable searches a company is required to undertake are obvious, and materiality and compliance costs are relevant factors to consider, a desire for simplifying compliance processes should not go so far as to undermine compliance with the requirement to use the most reliable available information. See paragraphs 1.57-1.58 on market differences and multi-country analyses for further detail of when local comparables are to be preferred.

47. It is not recommended, particularly at the stage of transfer pricing risk assessment, to require that the transfer pricing documentation should be certified by an outside auditor or other third party. Similarly, mandatory use of consulting firms to prepare transfer pricing documentation is not recommended.

E. Implementation and review

It is essential that the new guidance in this Chapter of the Guidelines, and particularly the new country-by-country report, be implemented effectively and consistently. It is the view of the OECD/G20 Project that taxpayers should deliver the local file directly to tax administrations in the relevant local jurisdiction. There are, however, different views about the filing process for the master file and the country-by-country report, and consequently about the mechanisms by which the information is to be made available to tax administrations in all relevant countries.

During the next several months, Working Party No. 6 of the Committee on Fiscal Affairs will undertake an analysis of potential mechanisms for filing and disseminating the master file and the country-by-country report. In considering potential filing and disseminating options for these documents, due regard will be given to:

- The importance of protecting the confidentiality of commercially sensitive information;
- The importance of making necessary information available to all relevant countries on a basis that will allow its timely use in transfer pricing risk assessment, thereby enhancing transparency for tax administrations;
- The importance of assuring that consistent financial information is

reported in all relevant countries in order to enhance MNE transparency for tax administrations;

- The importance of maintaining consistent reporting rules across countries as a means of limiting taxpayer compliance costs;

- The importance of assuring a common understanding for all relevant tax administrations of how the MNE operates;

- The importance of assuring that the information provided by taxpayers in relation to Annexes I – III will be used by tax administrations only for appropriate enforcement of transfer pricing rules;

- The importance that the development of effective phase-in rules may have for successfully transitioning to the new documentation regime; and

- The possible contributions that (i) treaty information exchange provisions, (ii) coordinated technological platforms, and (iii) the development of model local law provisions, may make to achieving the objectives of effective transfer pricing risk assessment in all relevant countries.

Because the mechanisms described in this Chapter are new and untested, there is a need to actively review their implementation. The transfer pricing documentation standards and country-by-country reporting standards will be revisited by countries participating in the BEPS project no later than the end of 2020 with a view to continuously improving the operation of those standards. In the course of the review, further consideration will be given to whether the documentation standards provide an adequate basis for transfer pricing risk assessment. Among other issues, active consideration will be given to whether additional transactional reporting of country-by-country or entity-by-entity payments of interest, royalties and especially service fees between associated enterprises should be required.

Annex I to Chapter V

Transfer pricing documentation – Master file

The following information should be included in the master file:

Organisational structure

- Chart illustrating the MNE's legal and ownership structure and geographical location of operating entities.

Description of MNE's business(es)

- General written description of the MNE's business including:
    - Important drivers of business profit;
    - A description of the supply chain for the group's five largest products and/or service offerings by turnover plus any other products and/or services amounting to more than 5 percent of group turnover. The required description could take the form of a chart or a diagram;
    - A list and brief description of important service arrangements between members of the MNE group, other than research and development (R&D) services, including a description of the capabilities of the principal locations providing important services and transfer pricing policies for allocating services costs and determining prices to be paid for intra-group services;
    - A description of the main geographic markets for the group's products and services that are referred to in the second bullet point above;
    - A brief written functional analysis describing the principal contributions to value creation by individual entities within the group, i.e. key functions performed, important risks

assumed, and important assets used;

- A description of important business restructuring transactions, acquisitions and divestitures occurring during the fiscal year.

MNE's intangibles (as defined in Chapter VI of these Guidelines)

- A general description of the MNE's overall strategy for the development, ownership and exploitation of intangibles, including location of principal R&D facilities and location of R&D management.
- A list of intangibles or groups of intangibles of the MNE group that are important for transfer pricing purposes and which entities legally own them.
- A list of important agreements among identified associated enterprises related to intangibles, including cost contribution arrangements, principal research service agreements and licence agreements.
- A general description of the group's transfer pricing policies related to R&D and intangibles.
- A general description of any important transfers of interests in intangibles among associated enterprises during the fiscal year concerned, including the entities, countries, and compensation involved.

MNE's intercompany financial activities

- A general description of how the group is financed, including important financing arrangements with unrelated lenders.
- The identification of any members of the MNE group that provide a central financing function for the group, including the country under whose laws the entity is organised and the place of effective management of such entities.
- A general description of the MNE's general transfer pricing policies related to financing arrangements between associated enterprises.

MNE's financial and tax positions

- The MNE's annual consolidated financial statement for the fiscal year concerned if otherwise prepared for financial reporting, regulatory, internal management, tax or other purposes.
- A list and brief description of the MNE group's existing unilateral advance pricing agreements (APAs) and other tax rulings relating to the allocation of income among countries.

Annex II to Chapter V

Transfer pricing documentation – Local file

The following information should be included in the local file:

Local entity

- A description of the management structure of the local entity, a local organisation chart, and a description of the individuals to whom local management reports and the country(ies) in which such individuals maintain their principal offices.
- A detailed description of the business and business strategy pursued by the local entity including an indication whether the local entity has been involved in or affected by business restructurings or intangibles transfers in the present or immediately past year and an explanation of those aspects of such transactions affecting the local entity.
- Key competitors.

Controlled transactions

For each material category of controlled transactions in which the entity is involved, provide the following information:

- A description of the material controlled transactions (e.g. procurement of manufacturing services, purchase of goods, provision of services, loans, financial and performance guarantees, licences of intangibles, etc.) and the context in which such transactions take place.
- The amount of intra-group payments and receipts for each category of controlled transactions involving the local entity (i.e. payments and receipts for products, services, royalties, interest, etc.) broken

down by tax jurisdiction of the foreign payor or recipient.

- An identification of associated enterprises involved in each category of controlled transactions, and the relationship amongst them.
- Copies of all material intercompany agreements concluded by the local entity.
- A detailed comparability and functional analysis of the taxpayer and relevant associated enterprises with respect to each documented category of controlled transactions, including any changes compared to prior years.1
- An indication of the most appropriate transfer pricing method with regard to the category of transaction and the reasons for selecting that method.
- An indication of which associated enterprise is selected as the tested party, if applicable, and an explanation of the reasons for this selection.
- A summary of the important assumptions made in applying the transfer pricing methodology.
- If relevant, an explanation of the reasons for performing a multi-year analysis.
- A list and description of selected comparable uncontrolled transactions (internal or external), if any, and information on relevant financial indicators for independent enterprises relied on in the transfer pricing analysis, including a description of the comparable search methodology and the source of such information.
- A description of any comparability adjustments performed, and an indication of whether adjustments have been made to the results of the tested party, the comparable uncontrolled transactions, or both.
- A description of the reasons for concluding that relevant transactions were priced on an arm's length basis based on the application of the

[1] To the extent this functional analysis duplicates information in the master file, a cross-reference to the master file is sufficient.

selected transfer pricing method.

- A summary of financial information used in applying the transfer pricing methodology.
- A copy of existing unilateral and bilateral/multilateral APAs and other tax rulings to which the local tax jurisdiction is not a party and which are related to controlled transactions described above.

Financial information

- Annual local entity financial accounts for the fiscal year concerned. If audited statements exist they should be supplied and if not, existing unaudited statements should be supplied.
- Information and allocation schedules showing how the financial data used in applying the transfer pricing method may be tied to the annual financial statements.
- Summary schedules of relevant financial data for comparables used in the analysis and the sources from which that data was obtained.

Annex III to Chapter V

A model template for the Country-by-Country Report

Table 1. Overview of allocation of income, taxes and business activities by tax jurisdiction

<table>
<tr><td colspan="11">Name of the MNE group:
Fiscal year concerned:</td></tr>
<tr><td rowspan="2">Tax Jurisdiction</td><td colspan="3">Revenues</td><td rowspan="2">Profit (Loss) Before Income Tax</td><td rowspan="2">Income Tax Paid (on cash basis)</td><td rowspan="2">Income Tax Accrued – Current Year</td><td rowspan="2">Stated capital</td><td rowspan="2">Accumulated earnings</td><td rowspan="2">Number of Employees</td><td rowspan="2">Tangible Assets other than Cash and Cash Equivalents</td></tr>
<tr><td>Unrelated Party</td><td>Related Party</td><td>Total</td></tr>
<tr><td></td><td></td><td></td><td></td><td></td><td></td><td></td><td></td><td></td><td></td><td></td></tr>
<tr><td></td><td></td><td></td><td></td><td></td><td></td><td></td><td></td><td></td><td></td><td></td></tr>
<tr><td></td><td></td><td></td><td></td><td></td><td></td><td></td><td></td><td></td><td></td><td></td></tr>
<tr><td></td><td></td><td></td><td></td><td></td><td></td><td></td><td></td><td></td><td></td><td></td></tr>
</table>

Table 2. List of all the Constituent Entities of the MNE group included in each aggregation per tax jurisdiction

Name of the MNE group: Fiscal year concerned:															
Tax Jurisdiction	Constituent Entities resident in the Tax Jurisdiction	Tax Jurisdiction of organisation or incorporation if different from Tax Jurisdiction of Residence	Main business activity(ies)												
			Research and Development	Holding or Managing intellectual property	Purchasing or Procurement	Manufacturing or Production	Sales, Marketing or Distribution	Administrative, Management or Support Services	Provision of Services to unrelated parties	Internal Group Finance	Regulated Financial Services	Insurance	Holding shares or other equity instruments	Dormant	Other[2]
	1.														
	2.														
	3.														
	1.														
	2.														
	3.														

[2] Please specify the nature of the activity of the Constituent Entity in the "Additional Information" section.

Table 3. Additional Information

Name of the MNE group: Fiscal year concerned:
Please include any further brief information or explanation you consider necessary or that would facilitate the understanding of the compulsory information provided in the country-by-country report.

General Instructions for Annex III to Chapter V

Purpose

This Annex III to Chapter V of these Guidelines contains a template for reporting a multinational enterprise's (MNE) allocation of income, taxes and business activities on a tax jurisdiction-by-tax jurisdiction basis. These instructions form an integral part of the model template for the country-by-country report.

Definitions

Reporting MNE

A Reporting MNE is the ultimate parent entity of an MNE group.

Constituent Entity

For purposes of completing Annex III, a Constituent Entity of the MNE group is any separate business unit of the MNE group (company, corporation, trust, partnership etc.) that is included in the consolidated group for financial reporting purposes. Entities excluded from financial statements only on size or materiality grounds should be included in the country-by-country report as Constituent Entities.

Treatment of Branches and Permanent Establishments

The term Constituent Entity also includes permanent establishments of a member of the MNE group conducting business in a tax jurisdiction, provided such permanent establishment prepares a separate income statement for regulatory purposes, financial reporting, internal management or tax purposes. The permanent establishment data should be reported by reference to the tax jurisdiction in which it is situated and not by reference to the tax jurisdiction of residence of the Constituent Entity of which the permanent establishment is a part. Residence tax jurisdiction reporting for the Constituent Entity of which the permanent establishment is a part should exclude financial data related to the permanent establishment.

Period covered by the annual template

The template should cover the fiscal year of the Reporting MNE. For Constituent Entities, at the discretion of the Reporting MNE, the template should reflect on a consistent basis either (i) information for the fiscal year of the relevant Constituent Entities ending on the same date as the fiscal year of the Reporting MNE, or ending within the 12 month period preceding such date, or (ii) information for all the relevant Constituent Entities reported for the fiscal year of the Reporting MNE.

Source of data

The Reporting MNE should consistently use the same sources of data from year to year in completing the template. The Reporting MNE may choose to use data from its consolidation reporting packages, from separate entity statutory financial statements, regulatory financial statements, or internal management accounts. It is not necessary to reconcile the revenue, profit and tax reporting in the template to the consolidated financial statements. If statutory financial statements are used as the basis for reporting, all amounts should be translated to the stated functional currency of the Reporting MNE at the average exchange rate for the year stated in the Additional Information section of the template. Adjustments need not be made, however, for differences in accounting principles applied from tax jurisdiction to tax jurisdiction.

The Reporting MNE should provide a brief description of the sources of data used in preparing the template in the Additional Information section of the template. If a change is made in the source of data used from year to year, the Reporting MNE should explain the reasons for the change and its consequences in the Additional Information section of the template.

Specific instructions for Annex III to Chapter V

Overview of allocation of income, taxes and business activities by tax jurisdiction (Table 1)

Tax Jurisdiction

In the first column of the template, the Reporting MNE should list all of the tax jurisdictions in which Constituent Entities of the MNE group are resident for tax purposes. A tax jurisdiction is defined as a State as well as a non-State jurisdiction which has fiscal autonomy. A separate line should be included for all Constituent Entities in the MNE group deemed by the Reporting MNE not to be resident in any tax jurisdiction for tax purposes. Where a Constituent Entity is resident in more than one tax jurisdiction, the applicable tax treaty tie breaker should be applied to determine the tax jurisdiction of residence. Where no applicable tax treaty exists, the Constituent Entity should be reported in the tax jurisdiction of the Constituent Entity's place of effective management. The place of effective management should be determined in accordance with the provisions of Article 4 of the OECD Model Tax Convention and its accompanying Commentary.

Revenues

In the three columns of the template under the heading Revenues, the reporting MNE should report the following information: (i) the sum of revenues of all the Constituent Entities of the MNE group in the relevant tax jurisdiction generated from transactions with associated enterprises; (ii) the sum of revenues of all the Constituent Entities of the MNE group in the relevant tax jurisdiction generated from transactions with independent parties; and (iii) the total of (i) and (ii). Revenues should include revenues from sales of inventory and properties, services, royalties, interest, premiums and any other amounts. Revenues should exclude payments received from other Constituent Entities that are treated as dividends in the payor's tax jurisdiction.

Profit (Loss) Before Income Tax

In the fifth column of the template, the Reporting MNE should report the sum of the profit (loss) before income tax for all the Constituent Entities resident for tax purposes in the relevant tax jurisdiction. The profit (loss) before income tax should include all extraordinary income and expense items.

Income Tax Paid (on Cash Basis)

In the sixth column of the template, the Reporting MNE should report the total amount of income tax actually paid during the relevant fiscal year by all the Constituent Entities resident for tax purposes in the relevant tax jurisdiction. Taxes paid should include cash taxes paid by the Constituent Entity to the residence tax jurisdiction and to all other tax jurisdictions. Taxes paid should include withholding taxes paid by other entities (associated enterprises and independent enterprises) with respect to payments to the Constituent Entity. Thus, if company A resident in tax jurisdiction A earns interest in tax jurisdiction B, the tax withheld in tax jurisdiction B should be reported by company A.

Income Tax Accrued (Current year)

In the seventh column of the template, the Reporting MNE should report the sum of the accrued current tax expense recorded on taxable profits or losses of the year of reporting of all the Constituent Entities resident for tax purposes in the relevant tax jurisdiction. The current tax expense should reflect only operations in the current year and should not include deferred taxes or provisions for uncertain tax liabilities.

Stated capital

In the eighth column of the template, the Reporting MNE should report the sum of the stated capital of all the Constituent Entities resident for tax purposes in the relevant tax jurisdiction. With regard to permanent establishments, the stated capital should be reported by the legal entity of which it is a permanent establishment unless there is a defined capital requirement in the permanent establishment tax jurisdiction for regulatory purposes.

Accumulated earnings

In the ninth column of the template, the Reporting MNE should report the sum of the total accumulated earnings of all the Constituent Entities resident for tax purposes in the relevant tax jurisdiction as of the end of the year. With regard to permanent establishments, accumulated earnings should be reported by the legal entity of which it is a permanent establishment.

Number of Employees

In the tenth column of the template, the Reporting MNE should report the total number of employees on a full-time equivalent (FTE) basis of all the Constituent Entities resident for tax purposes in the relevant tax jurisdiction. The number of employees may be reported as of the year-end, on the basis of average employment levels for the year, or on any other basis consistently applied across tax jurisdictions and from year to year. For this purpose, independent contractors participating in the ordinary operating activities of the Constituent Entity may be reported as employees. Reasonable rounding or approximation of the number of employees is permissible, providing that such rounding or approximation does not materially distort the relative distribution of employees across the various tax jurisdictions. Consistent approaches should be applied from year to year and across entities.

Tangible Assets other than Cash and Cash Equivalents

In the eleventh column of the template, the Reporting MNE should report the sum of the net book values of tangible assets of all the Constituent Entities resident for tax purposes in the relevant tax jurisdiction. With regard to permanent establishments, assets should be reported by reference to the tax jurisdiction in which the permanent establishment is situated. Tangible assets for this purpose do not include cash or cash equivalents, intangibles, or financial assets.

List of all the Constituent Entities of the MNE group included in each aggregation per tax jurisdiction (Table 2)

Constituent Entities resident in the Tax Jurisdiction

The Reporting MNE should list, on a tax jurisdiction-by-tax jurisdiction basis and by legal entity name, all the Constituent Entities of the MNE group which are resident for tax purposes in the relevant tax jurisdiction. As stated above with regard to permanent establishments, however, the permanent establishment should be listed by reference to the tax jurisdiction in which it is situated. The legal entity of which it is a permanent establishment should be noted (*e.g.* XYZ Corp – Tax Jurisdiction A PE).

Tax Jurisdiction of organisation or incorporation if different from Tax Jurisdiction of Residence

The Reporting MNE should report the name of the tax jurisdiction under whose laws the Constituent Entity of the MNE is organised or incorporated if it is different from the tax jurisdiction of residence.

Main business activity(ies)

The Reporting MNE should determine the nature of the main business activity(ies) carried out by the Constituent Entity in the relevant tax jurisdiction, by ticking one or more of the appropriate boxes.

Business activities
Research and Development
Holding or managing intellectual property
Purchasing or Procurement
Manufacturing or Production
Sales, Marketing or Distribution
Administrative, Management or Support Services
Provision of services to unrelated parties
Internal group finance
Regulated Financial Services
Insurance
Holding shares or other equity instruments
Dormant
Other[3]

[3] Please specify the nature of the activity of the Constituent Entity in the "Additional Information" section.

ORGANISATION FOR ECONOMIC CO-OPERATION AND DEVELOPMENT

The OECD is a unique forum where governments work together to address the economic, social and environmental challenges of globalisation. The OECD is also at the forefront of efforts to understand and to help governments respond to new developments and concerns, such as corporate governance, the information economy and the challenges of an ageing population. The Organisation provides a setting where governments can compare policy experiences, seek answers to common problems, identify good practice and work to co-ordinate domestic and international policies.

The OECD member countries are: Australia, Austria, Belgium, Canada, Chile, the Czech Republic, Denmark, Estonia, Finland, France, Germany, Greece, Hungary, Iceland, Ireland, Israel, Italy, Japan, Korea, Luxembourg, Mexico, the Netherlands, New Zealand, Norway, Poland, Portugal, the Slovak Republic, Slovenia, Spain, Sweden, Switzerland, Turkey, the United Kingdom and the United States. The European Union takes part in the work of the OECD.

OECD Publishing disseminates widely the results of the Organisation's statistics gathering and research on economic, social and environmental issues, as well as the conventions, guidelines and standards agreed by its members.

OECD PUBLISHING, 2, rue André-Pascal, 75775 PARIS CEDEX 16
(23 2014 30 1 P) ISBN 978-92-64-21922-9 – 2014-01

CPSIA information can be obtained
at www.ICGtesting.com
Printed in the USA
BVOW06s0035160817
491875BV00010BA/112/P

9 789264 219229